Return Of Military Dead Buried In France:
Hearings Before The Committee On Foreign
Affairs, House Of Representatives, Part 3

A. J. Montague

In the interest of creating a more extensive selection of rare historical book reprints, we have chosen to reproduce this title even though it may possibly have occasional imperfections such as missing and blurred pages, missing text, poor pictures, markings, dark backgrounds and other reproduction issues beyond our control. Because this work is culturally important, we have made it available as a part of our commitment to protecting, preserving and promoting the world's literature. Thank you for your understanding.

RETURN OF MILITARY DEAD BURIED IN FRANCE

HEARINGS

BEFORE THE

COMMITTEE ON FOREIGN AFFAIRS

HOUSE OF REPRESENTATIVES

SIXTY-SIXTH CONGRESS
FIRST SESSION

PART 3

NOVEMBER 13, 1919

STATEMENTS OF

Hon. A. J. MONTAGUE, M. C.; Hon. GEORGE WAYNE ANDERSON, of Richmond, Va., and members of delegation from Richmond; Rev. J. A. DUFF, of Pittsburgh, Pa., and members of delegation from Pittsburgh; Col. C. C. PIERCE, Q. M. C., War Department.

WASHINGTON
GOVERNMENT PRINTING OFFICE
1919

COMMITTEE ON FOREIGN AFFAIRS.

Sixty-sixth Congress,

FIRST SESSION.

STEPHEN G. PORTER, Pennsylvania, *Chairman*.

JOHN JACOB ROGERS, Massachusetts.
HENRY W. TEMPLE, Pennsylvania.
AMBROSE KENNEDY, Rhode Island.
EDWARD E. BROWNE, Wisconsin.
MERRILL MOORES, Indiana.
WILLIAM E. MASON, Illinois.
WALTER H. NEWTON, Minnesota.
L. J. DICKINSON, Iowa.
ERNEST R. ACKERMAN, New Jersey.
FRANK L. SMITH, Illinois.
JAMES T. BEGG, Ohio
ALANSON B. HOUGHTON, New York.

HENRY D. FLOOD, Virginia.
J. CHARLES LINTHICUM, Maryland.
WILLIAM S. GOODWIN, Arkansas.
CHARLES M. STEDMAN, North Carolina.
ADOLPH J. SABATH, Illinois.
J. WILLARD RAGSDALE, South Carolina.
GEORGE HUDDLESTON, Alabama.
TOM CONNALLY, Texas.
THOMAS F. SMITH, New York.

EDMUND F. ERK, *Clerk*.

RETURN OF MILITARY DEAD BURIED IN FRANCE.

COMMITTEE ON FOREIGN AFFAIRS,
HOUSE OF REPRESENTATIVES,
Thursday, November 13, 1919.

The committee met at 10.30 o'clock a. m., Hon. Stephen G. Porter (chairman), presiding.

The CHAIRMAN. Gentlemen, I called this meeting for the purpose of hearing a delegation from Richmond, Va., and one from Pittsburgh, Pa., on the question of the removal of the soldier dead from France, and before going into the hearing I would like to read into the record a letter from the Department of State to the American ambassador at Paris.

Mr. HUDDLESTON. Mr. Chairman, may I inquire how much time we are going to consume with this hearing? The bill which is now being considered on the floor is of very great importance.

The CHAIRMAN. I understand that, and I am going to limit it as much as I can.

Mr. HUDDLESTON. Is there a limit on the time?

The CHAIRMAN. Yes; I have practically limited it to an hour—30 minutes for the Richmond people, and 30 minutes for the Pittsburgh people.

Mr. HUDDLESTON. I was just going to say that reluctant as I would be to do so, I would feel compelled to object to extending it beyond one hour.

The CHAIRMAN. I realize that. I suppose you are interested in the labor section of the bill.

Mr. HUDDLESTON. Yes; we are interested in the whole bill.

The CHAIRMAN. I believe the committee understands that I have an arrangement with the State Department to file with this committee all communications passing between our Government and the French Government on this question, and this is the latest one and I would like to read into the record.

(Telegram from the Secretary of State to the American ambassador at Paris:)

DEPARTMENT OF STATE,
October 30, 1919.

In accordance with that part of agreement quoted in embassy's August 28, 1918, regarding military dead buried in France, the War Department desires to reach an understanding with the French Government by which present ministerial instructions prohibiting exhumation and transportation of military dead may be rescinded or modified in case of American dead so as to enable War Department to undertake as speedily as possible removal of bodies of American soldiers, where removal is desired by next of kin, in harmony with repeatedly announced policy of War Department. Notwithstanding apparently determined opposition of French Government, it is felt that our Government should do its utmost to keep faith with relatives of soldier dead.

The following reasons for exception in favor of America may be cited: (a) Great distance between France and America and expense involved make it impracticable for large majority of relatives to visit graves as can be done by those living in other allied countries. (b) Comparatively small number of American soldiers buried in France whose removal is desired by their next of kin. Of 4,500,000 soldier dead only 65,000 are American soldiers and of these next of kin do not desire in excess of 40,000 returned to America. (c) A large proportion of American dead are buried on or near battlefields and arrangements can probably be made to avoid transportation over any considerable portion of France, thus avoiding any great interference with traffic or creating depression in morale which seems principal reason for Government's opposition. (d) Arrangements being made for return of bodies from other countries numbering about 4,600. Such return will necessarily create toward France an unfavorable impression because of persistent refusal to allow similar action. (e) War Department influenced by agreement with French Government sent out inquiries to all next of kin to ascertain if return was desired. It would now be very embarrassing for War Department if it were compelled to inform relatives that France refuses to permit return of bodies, such information arousing resentment against France of relatives of Americans who gave their lives for freedom. In accordance with above you are instructed to make strongest representations possible to bring about such modification of present policy as will permit removal of American dead from France.

Mr. Montague, of Virginia, is here.

STATEMENT OF HON. A. J. MONTAGUE, A REPRESENTATIVE IN CONGRESS FROM THE STATE OF VIRGINIA.

Mr. MONTAGUE. Mr. Chairman, I will not take the time of the committee more than an instant. I wish you to hear the committee from the city of Richmond, Va.

Mr. Chairman, on October 24, I introduced a joint resolution which I beg to read:

That the War Department shall take appropriate action to exhume and return to the United States of America within six months after the passage of this resolution the bodies of all soldiers of the American Expeditionary Forces who died and are buried in France, and the return of whose bodies to America is desired and expressed by the nearest of kin.

SEC. 2. That the State Department shall cooperate with the War Department in effectuating the purposes of this resolution.

Then the next section carries the appropriation. This seems to have been referred to the military affairs committee and not to this committee. My purpose was to engage the cooperation of these two bodies, and especially did I embrace the foreign affairs department for the purpose of effectuating appropriate negotiations with the French Government, relieving any friction, and so forth.

As to the merits of the bill, permit me to say that I have no pride of opinion as to any bill, Mr. Chairman, and my resolution was drawn hurriedly, and back in my own mind I thought I should submit amendments as more thorough consideration might suggest.

I think, Mr. Chairman, this is vitally and fundamentally a personal question in its chief aspect. I think our Government should yield to that paramount, domestic consideration, namely, that the nearest kin of dead people should say what should be done with them. If they want them to remain in France, they should remain in France. If they want them to be brought here, they should be brought here. If I lost a child, it is a matter with me where the child should be buried, and I think the Government should effectuate the wishes when properly expressed. That is the outline thought, and I will not reinforce that by any argument. To my mind, it is so obvious that it needs no support.

The question of the practical execution of whatever resolution may be derived at by the Congress is a matter of moment. I did not name in my resolution any body except that the War Department and the Department of State should undertake this work. Upon more mature consideration, Mr. Chairman, I am of opinion, perhaps, that there should be a little more detail given, and I am inclined to think that a civil commission, perhaps with one person from the War Department and maybe one from the Navy Department—but I would have the majority of it a civil commission. In my own view, it should be a commission without salary. I would name some of the fathers who would be only too glad to perform a service of this sort without pay, only their full expenses provided for. Then I think you would have the work done. This committee has had experiences with commissions. I am not criticising commissions; I have had the misfortune, or good fortune, to have been upon several myself, but only one or two people, as a rule, do the work of a commission, and they hang on and hang on until time is consumed. Expedition is one of the chief elements in the merit of this undertaking. Whatever is done ought to be done reasonably speedily.

Now, Mr. Chairman, I will ask you to hear Col. George Wayne Anderson, of the city of Richmond, Va., who is very vitally interested in this matter; personally interested, having lost a son in the Expeditionary Forces, who is now in France.

Mr. HUDDLESTON. Mr. Chairman, may I suggest that at the instance of Gov. Montague we allot the hour among those who wish to be heard.

The CHAIRMAN. The half hour, Mr. Huddleston, because there is also a delegation here from Pittsburgh.

Mr. HUDDLESTON. Would it not be better to allot that time?

The CHAIRMAN. Yes; if Gov. Montague will do that.

Mr. MONTAGUE. I think the chairman can do that. I am on the committee that reports this railroad bill to the House, and for that reason I am constrained to vote, and I have explained to my friends from Richmond that I will have to leave in a very few moments. I do not think these gentlemen will take long. Col. Anderson, you will not want half an hour.

Mr. ANDERSON. No, sir; I think not.

Mr. HUDDLESTON. I suggest the gentlemen agree among themselves.

The CHAIRMAN. All right; proceed, Col. Anderson.

STATEMENT OF HON. GEORGE WAYNE ANDERSON, ASSISTANT CITY ATTORNEY, RICHMOND, VA.

The CHAIRMAN. Colonel, will you state your full name, address, occupation, and the organization, if any, which you represent.

Mr. ANDERSON. My name is George Wayne Anderson; I am assistant city attorney of the city of Richmond, Va. I represent a voluntary association of some 125 parents and relatives in Richmond, which association has met and adopted resolutions and memorials and a petition both to the President of the United States and both branches of Congress, which have been presented by that committee in person, as well as to the Secretary of War. Fifty odd of the parents in Richmond signed those resolutions, which must be in the archives of the House somewhere, calling for the return of their sons during the present winter, if possible. We considered that it could be done during the present winter, and the sooner the better. The committee should understand that we parents are by the present method of procedure by the War Department being compelled to look forward to some indefinite time in the future when our sons' bodies will be brought back to us, and we will have a funeral in our families. It is a matter we want to get behind us. Our wives want those bodies. They want to visit those graves. We desire them for reasons which we set out in this petition, and I have here copies of the resolutions which we have adopted, as well as some of the reasons, which I will file without stopping to read them.

(The papers referred to follow:)

MEMORANDUM OF FACTS RELATING TO THE RETURN TO AMERICA OF THE AMERICAN DEAD IN FRANCE, PREPARED AND ADOPTED BY THE EXECUTIVE COMMITTEE APPOINTED BY A MEETING OF MORE THAN 100 RELATIVES OF THOSE WHO GAVE THEIR LIVES, HELD AT RICHMOND, VA.

I. Fifty-odd of the parents and nearest kin of Richmond boys who lie buried in France signed resolutions asking for the return of their sons' bodies to America during the coming winter, and presented these resolutions to the President and the Congress as well as to the Secretary of War. They have heard nothing from the President, and nothing has been done by Congress, but the Secretary of War informed their committee that although the Government intended to keep its promise to return to America the bodies of those whose parents insisted upon it, the department had no present plans looking to that end, but that it had ample funds and still controlled the necessary shipping. He very frankly said the Government thought these bodies should be allowed to remain in France forever, and hoped that the number of parents who would insist upon their return to America would diminish as time passed.

The Secretary further said that he would refuse to give the consent of the War Department to any parent who desired to visit France and bring back a son's remains at private expense, and even if such parent obtained the consent of the French Government that he would feel obliged to interpose an objection.

The committee, which called on him, understood his reasons for this attitude to be substantially as follows:

First. That two laws were pending in the French Chamber of Deputies forbidding the removal of any body from France for a period of two and three years, respectively, from and after January 1, 1919;

That our Government had protested against the passage of either law, but that such removal was now forbidden by some executive regulation issued by the French Government;

That the reason for this was the inability of the French Government to comply with the request of French parents who were demanding the return of their sons to their home localities, and it was thought the morale of the French people would be destroyed if the French Government should undertake the return to such localities of the 1,700,000 French dead, with consequent funerals in every hamlet of France lasting through a probable period of six months, thereby causing a renewed outburst of mourning and withdrawing the attention of the people from productive employment so necessary at present to the life of France;

That to consent to such removal by America of Americans would lead to similar demands by England, Italy, Belgium, and other nations, and that no French Government could stand which granted such privileges to other countries and refused them to the French.

To this we say that it is well understood that England, Italy, Belgium, and other countries have avowed the policy of leaving their dead permanently in France; that none of them began the war with a distinct promise that such bodies should be returned, as did America, and none of them took such precautions to insure identity of the dead as did America.

As for the French, we believe that generous people would gladly acquiesce in seeing American parents enjoy this privilege even if denied to themselves, if a representation was made to them that American boys left homes 3,000 miles away and crossed the seas to give their lives for France and her cause; that American parents could not visit their graves, and that to refuse consent would merely cause prolonged suffering, distress, and sorrow to such parents as were resolved sooner or later to have their sons brought home, and would cause such parents to look forward for years to the sorrowful event of the reburial of their sons, and deprive them meantime of the comfort and consolation to be derived from the knowledge that their remains were at home and under their own loving care.

We say further that the original promise of the Government was that all such bodies would be returned unless parents objected; whereas, now the promise reads that none will be returned unless the parents insist. The time to redeem this promise is now while the Government is winding up the war and still controls the necessary funds and shipping. The enforced delay can only cause distress to parents who are resolved in this matter and result in the coercion of many against their will as well as in dulling the force of the promise and probably compelling such parents to become petitioners to some future Congress for the necessary appropriation.

No such delay was expressed or fairly implied in the promise of our Government. As for the French Government we feel sure it will yield to any firm request of our country on this subject, and that the French people will support it in doing so.

Second. It is said that our boys would wish to lie where they fell in foreign soil upon the scene of their great sacrifice.

We think this is absolutely untrue. Our boys went to France knowing of the Government promise that their bodies would be returned, and we do not and can not believe that one American boy out of 10,000 would have failed to say, if asked, that he would prefer to rest in his native land. To them France itself was almost an abstraction. The love in their hearts was for America, and the crusaders' spirit was roused in them by German atrocity and inhumanity. Many had never left their native States, and we feel sure that their desire would be to find a resting place in America.

Third. It is said that their bodies will be well cared for in beautiful cemeteries for all time.

Our answer is that so may they be cared for for all time in American cemeteries, and we call to witness America's memorial day for the heroes of other wars.

We say further that these foreign cemeteries lie in the direct path of invasion along which hostile armies have tread since a time before the Christian era, and along which for topographical reasons, they must forever tread in all time to come. If like Patrick Henry, we judge the future by the past, another German invasion of the west is a certainty, and with it the destruction of our cemeteries is a certainty. Our own land is the land of peace and justice. There and not along the war highways of France may be found perpetual peace and rest.

Fourth. We are told that our boys should be left in France as a heroic and appealing monument to the services of our country and the love it has for the principles of justice and human freedom.

To this we say that our services to mankind were really more spiritual than material; that the great fact of the sacrifice of our sons' lives is the appealing memorial, and not their crumbling bodies; that not one Frenchman out of tens of thousands will ever see their graves, and that we do not wish our sons' graves to be viewed by idle tourists or to be used as a source of profit by the French people.

Fifth. Another reason alleged is of a sanitary nature, and it is said that the lives of the living might be imperiled, and yet our country has been busy from armistice day until now exhuming and transporting the bodies of our dead from the fields of battle, on which they gave their lives, to concentration cemeteries at Romagne and other places. Surely any possible peril existed then and not now after the lapse of a year.

In short, we have done the very thing it is said must not be done, and it is not true that our boys now lie where they fell or in the graves in which their comrades placed them.

Sixth. It is said that the task will be great and that confusion may result. The task will be great, but confusion should not result and will not result, except in few cases, if the Graves Registration Service faithfully performed its task as we believe it did. Our boys had duplicate identification tags about their necks, and except in rare cases those tags still remain upon their bodies. Reasonable care in placing them in well marked caskets will prevent confusion in transportation and insure certain and safe delivery.

We learn that these bodies were reinterred in flimsy wooden coffins of material often unfit for such purpose, and were carelessly and imperfectly put together. Removal now can be certain of identity, but delay for years multiplies the danger of confusion.

II. That we are right in wishing our sons' bodies brought home, and that such a wish is the natural cry of the human heart is proved, first, by the original promise of our country that such should be the case; second, by the cry of French parents for the return of their sons from the battle fields on which they lie; third, by the instinct of our own hearts; and fourth, by the action of England in returning the bodies of Edith Cavell and Capt. Fryatt, as well as that of our own country in the Spanish War. Our national cemeteries also attest the fact.

Many parents desire to bring back home at their own expense the bodies of their sons, and are willing to make the pecuniary sacrifice involved. The fact that others are unable so to do is not a sufficient or just reason for refusing them permission, though it is sufficient to stir our Government to action.

The undersigned citizens of Richmond, Va., in meeting assembled, speaking for themselves alone, after due consideration and proper deliberation, adopt the following resolutions:

1. We have confidently relied upon our country's promise that the bodies of our dead, who gave their lives in the great war, would be unmistakably identified and safely returned to their native land.

2. We have heard and considered the reasons, both practical and sentimental, that have been urged against the return of these bodies to America, by Gen. Pershing and by others, and we are not unmindful of the mourning and the grief of France, for we also bear the heavy cross. But upon full consideration and after due deliberation we still desire that our dead be returned to us that they may sleep amid the ashes of their fathers, and give solace to our declining years through the visitation and care of their graves.

3. Our country's promise did not contain or fairly imply a delay of three years in such return, and to prolong our present state will but increase our sorrows and result, we fear, in a final failure to realize our desires.

4. We have kept the faith to the uttermost, and we now respectfully memorialize the President and the Congress of our country to keep the faith with us, and to bring about the return of our sacred dead to the land they loved during the coming winter at the latest.

5. In view of the uncertainty of our present state we recommend to all parents and relatives of those who died abroad, who think and feel as we do, whether resident in Virginia or in other States, that they hold meetings and adopt resolutions expressing their wishes and memorializing the President and Congress upon the subject they have at heart.

Let me say, Mr. Chairman and gentlemen of the committee, that we originally desired the War Department to act in this matter. We have interviewed the Secretary of War. I, myself, have interviewed him more than once. I have always been treated courteously and with the utmost frankness. In May he told me that I might confidently rely upon having my son returned to me last summer. In September he told me they had no present plans and no dates, and he frankly told me they did not want to bring the bodies back; that he did not think they ought to be brought back; that it would be a great task, and they thought the parents ought to consent to a still greater sacrifice and leave those bodies forever in France, but that the Government intended to keep its promise and would bring back the bodies of those whose parents insisted upon it. My experience in life is that when a man does not want to do a thing it is always easy to find reasons for not doing anything. For that reason we have changed our view and do not think the War Department is the proper body to act in this matter, as a department, simply for the reason they do not want to do it, and they frankly say they do not want to do it. They do not think it ought to be done, and they frankly say they do not think it ought to be done.

We believe that Col. Pierce, the chief of the Graves Registration Service, does think it ought to be done, and realizes the promise that the Government has made, not only to us but to our sons. They carried their promise around their necks in the shape of duplicate tags, and every movement they made made the promise touch their bodies. Every boy went to France with the promise of the Government about his neck that his body should be brought back, and they say they are perfectly willing to do it, but do not want to do it. Col. Pierce is perfectly willing to do it and does want to do it. We think that if this committee could authorize him to proceed at once that that would be the best way to do it.

We see no reason why it should not be done during the coming winter. If, however, the committee takes up the Bland bill and determines to proceed upon lines of that character, we are very anxious to see at least two amendments. The Bland bill now names January 1, 1922, as the date upon which the return and reburial of these bodies must be completed. That, you will observe, is exactly the three years that the French Government demand, from 1919 to 1922. We do not think we ought to consent to 1922. We would like to see that bill amended, if it is to be adopted, to make it January 1, 1921, giving the whole of the next year to this task if that bill is to be adopted.

We would like to see another amendment made, and that is an amendment authorizing parents who desire to bring their sons back at their own expense and under their own supervision without any Government aid at all, except moral and legal—we would like to see an amendment authorizing that to be done and requiring the War Department and the State Department to give such parents every support that is necessary and the hearty support of our Government in bringing these bodies back. I think, Mr. Chairman, I can say that that is the program we would like to see carried out.

The resolution of Mr. Montague meets with our unqualified approval, except we doubt whether the War Department, as a department, is sufficient. We would like to see Col. Pierce designated as the man to do this work, and six months' time we think ought to be sufficient. If that is not sufficient, certainly next year ought to be sufficient.

Now, as to the French people, we sympathize with them; but they are demanding of their Government precisely what we are asking of ours. We are asking of ours not only what they ask of theirs but what our Government promised us, and what their Government did not promise them. If it comes down to a matter of the feelings of the American parents and the feelings of the French people, we think our Government ought to stand with the American parents and insist to the French Government that these boys who crossed 3,000 miles of sea to give their lives to the French cause, where their parents can never visit their graves, that they must yield to our demand that we be allowed to bring these bodies back. We have no confidence whatever in there being no further wars, and we note with great anxiety that these cemeteries are placed right in the highway of war. Lines of warfare are fixed by the configuration of the earth's surface, and from the time of the Christian era Julius Cæsar was fighting these Germans right along the Meuse Valley where our great Romagne Cemetery has been placed. The war again ravished that territory in 1870, and it did so again in this war, and it will do so again in the next war for the reason that there is no way for the Germans to get at the French except through the Meuse Valley and through Belgium, and our cemeteries will lie right in the path of any future war and will certainly be destroyed.

We think our own country is the land of peace and justice, and we think that there alone on the face of this earth can a man have perpetual rest and peace. Our avowed policy for all time has been to bury our soldier dead in national cemeteries and to care for them. They can be just as well cared for here as in France and we think better, and for our part we do not desire to have our sons made a show where idle tourists will go and French people make money carrying them there and have them be a spectacle. We think the services of our country to the world were really, essentially spiritual, notwithstanding the material service we performed. We do not think one Frenchman out of ten thousand will bear in his heart any gratitude to us by seeing one of these graves. It will be on account of the great fact that our sons went there and gave their lives and not by reason of their bodies being in French soil. That fact is one which will ever remain, and that is the monument to our country.

Something has been said to us about it being a badge of nobility to us to have our sons in this cemetery. We think that is nonsense. It is no glory to us that our sons gave their lives. It is glory to them, and the fact that our son is buried in the Romagne cemetery adds no nobility to me, and it is nonsense to tell me it does.

Another thing said to us is that the boys would want to stay there. We think that is absolutely untrue. Those boys, as I have said, went with this promise about their necks that they would be brought home. To them France itself was an abstraction. There was not 1 man out of 100 in America who knew anything of France except the name. They went to France upon the call of their own country and for love of their own country and because in their hearts the spirit of the crusader was spurred by the atrocities of the German people, and they went there to put an end to that forever, if they could. They did not go there from any love of France. It was a mere sentimental addition. The call of duty to them was the call of America and the love in their hearts was the love of America and of humanity. They did not go there for France and they did not want to lie in France. I do not believe anybody but a nomad would. I do not think 1 boy out of 100,000 Americans would have hesitated a minute if asked where he wanted to be buried in case he was killed. If he had been asked, he would have said that he wanted to be brought home. I have it from the major commanding the Richmond battalion, which distinguished itself in the Meuse fighting, that every single man in that battalion told him. "Major, if I am killed, I want my body brought home to Virginia." Every one of them told him that. Therefore, we think it is talk and nothing but talk to say that these boys would want to stay there. They are not lying where their comrades placed them. They have been taken up and reburied. My boy was buried in a cemetery with 300 bodies, and every last one of them has been exhumed and carried over and reinterred in Romagne. They are not lying where their comrades placed them. They have already been disturbed, and we think they ought to be brought back.

It is said to us that sanitary reasons will prevent. If sanitary reasons would apply at all in this great devasted region, where there is absolutely no settlement and practically no inhabitants, they would have applied when they were exhumed and reinterred in Romagne and not now, a year after they have been dead. We see no reason in the world why those bodies should not be hermetically sealed upon this cemetery field with perfect security to the health of the people. There is not a man in France within a radius of a mile of the Romagne Cemetery and there is nobody's health there to be imperiled.

Mr. DICKINSON. Mr. Chairman, I would like to ask one question, if Col. Anderson will permit.

Mr. ANDERSON. Certainly.

Mr. DICKINSON. Would you be in favor of this committee giving any consideration to the action of the national meeting of the American Legion of the World War Veterans in passing the resolution which they seem to be favorably considering that the soldier dead should be allowed to remain in France?

Mr. ANDERSON. I would not, Mr. Dickinson if you please, for the reason that it would be a violation of the expressed pledge of this Government to the boys themselves and to the parents of those boys. I would favor giving any proper consideration to any resolution passed by the legion that did not violate a pledge of the Government.

Mr. FLOOD. The wishes of the nearest of kin of these soldiers who died over there are more to be considered than the wishes of their comrades.

Mr. ANDERSON. I think so. I think we have certain legal rights. The moment we declare peace with Germany, what legal right has the Government to deny me the right to have my boy's body. They are keeping it against my will. As soon as we are at peace, why have I not the right to demand it and enforce my demand, if you consider the question of legal right?

Mr. FLOOD. Colonel, I want to say that I concur in everything you say except as to the attitude of the War Department, I think the fixed attitude of the War Department now is to bring these bodies back as soon as they can do so without a disagreeable encounter with the French Government. When that will be I do not know.

Mr. ANDERSON. The impression I got from the War Department was that the Secretary was very kind to me and very courteous, but he told me frankly that he did not think these bodies ought to be brought back.

Mr. FLOOD. At one time that was the Secretary's opinion, as I understood.

Mr. ANDERSON. He hoped the lapse of time would diminish the number of parents who insisted upon it, but said they would at some indefinite time, unknown and unsettled and unfixed, comply with the promise if we insisted upon it. The promise was that they were going to be brought back unless we said we did not want them brought back.

Mr. FLOOD. You know that in order to find out the wishes of the parents or nearest of kin they sent out a questionnaire?

Mr. ANDERSON. Yes.

Mr. FLOOD. And three-fourths of the parties who were authorized to speak asked the War Department to bring these bodies back, and I understand that that fixes the policy of the War Department definitely.

Mr. ANDERSON. Mr. Flood, we are not disputing the fact that the War Department will loyally abide by the promise at some indefinite time in the future. Our only desire now is to fix some time when they will act. I am not arraigning the War Department, except I do think that parents who desire their sons brought back and who are resolved on it are being held up because of considerations for the French people, and in the hope that a great many of them will abandon the desire to have their sons brought back, which will diminish the number that will be brought back. I do not see why I should not be allowed to go there and bring my son back to-morrow—that is what I want to do—at my own expense and under my own supervision. I do not want the Government——

Mr. FLOOD. I do not think the Government has considered the money end of it. The Government is able to bring them back.

Mr. ANDERSON. I do not think so, either. The Secretary told me that they had plenty of money and plenty of ships.

Mr. CONNALLY. I want to say, Col. Anderson, that I am entirely in sympathy with your objects in view, but just on this one point: Do you contend that the Government of the United States could require this unless it was done under an arrangement with the French Government?

Mr. ANDERSON. No. I realize perfectly the police powers of the French Government.

Mr. CONNALLY. It seems to me that so far as our discussions here are concerned that the only question before the committee is securing from the French Government some arrangement by which we can do this. I do not think there is any sentiment in this committee at all adverse to bringing back the bodies of every American soldier whose family desires that body returned. That question, and the question as to the instrumentality which will be employed in returning them are the only questions, I think, that this committee is really concerned with seriously at all.

Mr. ANDERSON. And the time, if I may suggest, Mr. Connally.

Mr. CONNALLY. Yes; of course, the time, and I think on that the committee is absolutely agreed that the earliest possible moment that that can be accomplished is to be desired.

Mr. ANDERSON. I would not wish to be understood as arraigning the War Department in any way, although I do not wish to diminish one jot what I say as to their not wanting to do this thing. They do not think it ought to be done. They have no present idea of when it will be done, and I think when a man does not want to do a thing and does not think it ought to be done, that it is always easy to find reasons why it can not be done.

Mr. CONNALLY. Not impugning your estimate of fairness at all, is not this a fairer estimate of the situation, that the War Department thinks it better, on the whole, that these bodies be permitted to remain in France, but that it intends to bring back every body whose family desires it returned.

Mr. ANDERSON. I think that is absolutely right, Mr. Connally. They intend to bring back every such body.

Mr. CONNALLY. Do you not concede, that however the War Department might think on this question, if this committee should pass a resolution somewhat like Gov. Montague's resolution directing that this be done, the War Department would have no alternative but to comply.

Mr. ANDERSON. I think so, as soon as the French Government would permit.

The CHAIRMAN. You believe, as I understand it, that the War Department does not think that these bodies should be brought home, and that, therefore, they are throwing all the obstacles they can in the way of bringing them home?

Mr. ANDERSON. I would not like to put it as strongly as that, or to say that they are throwing obstacles in the way, but I would say that there is an unwillingness or unreadiness to act.

Mr. FLOOD. I think that attitude of unwillingness on the part of the department has changed since the responses were received to the questionnaire.

Mr. ANDERSON. We saw them in September.

The CHAIRMAN. The attitude of the War Department has entirely changed within the last few months.

Mr. FLOOD. Gen. March, the Chief of Staff, appeared before this committee some months ago, and stated his attitude as being in favor of the return of the bodies.

Mr. MONTAGUE. Mr. B. A. Cleary, of Richmond, who also lost a son, will address the committee.

STATEMENT OF MR. BERNARD A. CLEARY, RICHMOND, VA.

Mr. CLEARY. Mr. Chairman and gentlemen of the committee, I not only lost a son, but an only son and only child. He was a young lieutenant, 21 years of age. I am not a speaker, and I can hardly express my thoughts. I will take only a few minutes of your time. You gentlemen are very busy, and perhaps do not have the time to think of these things as we, to whom they are so vital, think of them. Col. Anderson has very admirably covered the ground, and there is little that I can add to the discussion. If the War Department wants to do the proper thing, or wants to bring these bodies back, they can bring them back, and if you gentlemen will do the nice thing they will bring them back. We have legal rights in this matter, and sooner or later we will get the bodies of our soldier dead. But if you gentlemen want to do the nice thing, you will speed them up. Let us have them while there is something left to bring back. Do not wait for 3 years, 5 years, or 10 years. We want those bodies now.

No man has the right to tell me what disposition I shall make of my boy's body. I have no right to tell you or any other man what disposition you shall make of the body of your child or of any member of your family. You recognize that fact, and everyone recognizes it. Now, gentlemen, there has been a great deal of talk about the insurmountable obstacles in the way of bringing those bodies home, but, as Col. Anderson has said, where there is a will there is a way. Do you gentlemen feel that the obstacles are insurmountable? I know that there are many contractors in this country who would be perfectly willing to undertake this job, and they could bring all of those bodies back inside of six months. Gentlemen, I am no speaker, but before I conclude I want to say a word in reference to this Bland bill, which, I think, is really of no service to us at all. To save my life, I can not see how it can be of any service to us in its present form, unless it is radically amended and changed. I do not agree to the idea of putting off the bringing of those bodies home until after two years, and I had just as soon not have any legislation as that. Besides, it provides that this commission shall ascertain the wishes of the relatives of the deceased soldiers. Why should we go over all that again? We have already got that information, and why should we go over that again? I think that about 71 per cent of the relatives of the deceased soldiers have already signified their desire to have these bodies brought back.

Gentlemen, I thank you for your attention.

The CHAIRMAN. Is there anybody else from Richmond who desires to be heard?

STATEMENT OF MR. E. WEBER HOHEN, RICHMOND, VA.

Mr. HOHEN. Mr. Chairman, I simply wish to say that I lost my only child in the war. The ground has been covered by Col. Anderson thoroughly, and he has expressed my wishes entirely.

I thank you.

The CHAIRMAN. There are a number of people here from Pittsburgh who would like to be heard, and I will first call on Rev. J. A. Duff.

STATEMENT OF REV. J. A. DUFF, PITTSBURGH, PA.

Mr. DUFF. Mr. Chairman, I appreciate the fact that the committee is reluctant on account of other important business to hear us at any length, and I appreciate the fact, also, Mr. Chairman, that the ground has been very well covered by those who have preceded me, and that it would be superfluous to go over that ground again. The position that we take has been so well stated, and, I might say, so eloquently and convincingly stated, that I hardly think it is necessary for me to now attempt to go over that ground again. I shall say only a few words, because there are others here from Pittsburgh who have had allotted to them some part of this time, and I have only a few minutes at any rate. I feel, Mr. Chairman, in a strange position, as being obliged to vindicate one of the oldest human instincts, and one that I supposed to be indisputable as such, in justifying my own feeling as a parent in this matter. Now, this is no imputation upon people who take the other position, if they do not invade the freedom of my own sentiment in the expression of this old human instinct, because some of the nicest people and some of my best friends, and some of those who have expressed the warmest degree of sympathy with my sorrow, have, as a matter of fact, undertaken to tell me how I ought to feel about this matter.

That is really what we are encountering in this propaganda that we are now making throughout the country, because there are a lot of good American people who think that they know better than we do, who have suffered the loss, how we ought to feel about it, and who say that we ought to be satisfied to have the bodies of our boys to stay over there in France where they will be well taken care of. I do not dispute the statement that they will be well taken care of, because I do not know, but that is something that we are up against. Now, as a matter of fact, I agree perfectly with what has been said— that is, that we are the only persons who have the right to say how we ought to feel about this matter. Not only should we be permitted to have our own sentiments about the matter of the disposal of our own dead, but we ought to be allowed to have the way cleared so that we may work out such sentiments and discharge the last rites ourselves. I have been pastor of one church for 40 years, and I have come in contact with a great many people who have had to deal sometimes with troublesome questions regarding the disposition of their dead. They have had to bring them home from California and Canada. One of the members of my church spent several thousand dollars trying to recover the body of a son who was drowned in Lake Muskegon.

There are some good people who might say that was a foolish thing to do. In this unfamiliar situation in which I have been placed in trying to express an instinct as old as Jacob and as old as Joseph, I sometimes wonder whether I am not, after all, too romantic or even Quixotic, or certainly too sentimental. A great many people seem to have that idea, but these are our boys, and we have suffered the loss, and the Government of the United States, as well as everybody else in the United States should give us the privilege of clinging to our own ideas as to what is the proper feeling. If we were allowed that privilege, there would be no question whatever as to the other matter. In view of the promise that our Government made, the promise that was made when our boys went over there, and on which promise they relied as a part of the comfort they felt in leaving their beloved ones, we have a right to express and realize our own feelings about the matter. We have the right to have what we want of the Government as our agent. The Government is not an agency to state the case of France and emphasize her attitude, but the Government is our agent to secure for us the bodies of our dead—the bodies of our boys who have made the supreme sacrifice for the Government, and whose bodies now belong to us. Every agency of the Government ought to be set in operation in order to fulfill that promise as expeditiously as possible. As a matter of fact, I am not arraigning the War Department, but we are entitled to that consideration.

In my own experience, I had a son who was a chaplain at general headquarters, at Chaumont, and when he came home he told me of the propaganda here under our very eyes. I do not criticize the War Department, but I do say this, that Gen. Pershing cabled the War Department saying that it would be a great thing to use the bodies of our dead—I am not quoting him properly, and I will commence again. His cablegram was to the effect that it would be in the interest of international sentiment and of cementing the bonds already existing between the Allies if the bodies of our dead should remain over there. They propose to use our dead. After they have given their lives, they are to be used to further foster international sentiment. I had a nephew, a major, who visited the grave of my boy, and who was at the dedication of the Romaigne Cemetery, and he told me that all of the signs, all the atmosphere, and all the tendency of what was said was to the effect that the cemeteries were to be permanent. I do not see how there can be any question as to the reluctance of the War Department to fulfill the promise of the Government.

Now, as to the boys' sentiment, that Col. Anderson was talking about, what was the sentiment of the boys? My own boy was not a weakly, sentimental man. I may be allowed to say that he was a lawyer in practice, and he was a man of strong personality. He was the left guard at Princeton the year they beat Yale and Harvard. He was that kind of a fellow. He was coach at Princeton, and a man of extraordinary strong personality. Of course, no one knows what the fortunes of war will be, and we had the understanding when he went away that his body would be brought back if he fell, and that was a part of the comfort he gave to us, that his body would be brought back. I simply mention that as an instance in order to express what I am sure was the general sentiment of the boys. Now, what right has the War Department or any department of the Government to be reluctant, or to take into consideration what France may want. I might say that that is a matter of diplomacy, but I think that if this committee is in favor of doing this thing, it should be done as expeditiously as possible, before many of the mothers and fathers are dead. A good many of them are old, and they are passing away. In fact, many of the fathers and mothers have already passed away. They want to have the bodies of their boys brought back now, and not after they are in their graves, but that is what will happen if things go on as they are now. I do not know whether this committee has the power or not, but if it has it ought to authorize the State Department, because the War Department is reluctant to act, and has said so, to take speedy action.

The Secretary of War, for example, has expressed, to Mr. Foster, sympathy with what Gen. Pershing said. It was in a letter, and it is stated in black and white. Of course, it would be going too far to say what you ought to do, but the chairman has asked for suggestions and I think that the thing for this committee to do, if you want to express the feelings of those who have suffered the loss, is to ask the State Department to proceed at once to negotiate for the return of the bodies in cases where the next of kin want them. Of course, we respect the feelings of those who do not want them, and we concede their right to say that. You should hurry the matter up so that half of those who are immediately concerned shall not be dead before the bodies are brought home. I see no reason in the world why those bodies should not be brought home this winter.

I have already taken up too much of your time.

Mr. DICKINSON. Have you any opinion to express as to whether or not Congress should make any provision that those bodies when brought home should be buried in a large national cemetery, or whether they should be put at the disposal of the relatives of the dead?

Mr. DUFF. The promise was to put them at the disposal of the families.

Mr. DICKINSON. You think that is the desire?

Mr. DUFF. Yes, sir; I think that is the desire, and I think that would be doing justice in the matter. Of course, if any parents think otherwise, I concede to them the right to think so.

The CHAIRMAN. If any bodies are unclaimed, do you think they should be buried in the National Cemetery at Arlington?

Mr. DUFF. Yes, sir. My position is this, that I have no right to say as to what any parent shall do or say, but my position is that those of us who do want the bodies, have a right to them. I am not a lawyer, and I can not say what our legal rights are, but we certainly have a natural right to them. They are our property, and if France for any reason should be disposed to hold them there, it is the business of our Government, it seems to me, and clearly the business of our Government, to tell them that they can not do that. If you allow me just one more word, I would like to say that there is a rising sentiment in this country on this subject. I wrote an article for The Presbyterian, and I have heard from it all over the country. It was very mild statement, with none of the directness of these statements to-day. All over the country they want to form leagues, and I got a letter last night from the pastor of the Presbyterian Church at Parkersburg, W. Va., asking how they should start a league. The Government will soon discover the attitude of hostility and resentment on the part of thousands of parents, and their propaganda will go out from those homes and will be something to be reckoned with. Loving France as I do, I do hope that France will see her way clear to do the proper thing in this matter. If not, we ought to be able to show her clearly that if she persists in saying that we must wait two years, she will stir up a sentiment in this country of such a character that the next time France is imperiled, she will have to reckon with the permanent hostility of all those people whom she has deprived of their natural rights.

Mr. DICKINSON. Do you think this committee should give consideration to the sentiment of the soldier boys themselves, in the American Legion of World War Veterans, so far as the disposition of the bodies is concerned?

Mr. DUFF. An outsider may believe that he knows better than we do how we ought to feel. I think the trouble with the American Legion——

Mr. DICKINSON (interposing). I am entirely in accord and sympathy with your views.

Mr. DUFF. I would not pay any attention to them unless they agreed with us. That is not a narrow view to take, for the simple reason that they have not thought the thing out and do not know how we feel. Do you recall what Shakespeare said? A man's house was burned and his wife and children were killed. A friend went to see him and said, "You must bear it like a man." The reply was, "I shall do so, but I must also feel it like a man." The friend did not understand feeling. He understood fortitude, but he did not understand feeling.

I thank you for your attention.

STATEMENT OF MR. J. D. FOSTER, CHAIRMAN OF BRING HOME THE DEAD SOLDIER LEAGUE, McKEESPORT, PA.

The CHAIRMAN. Mr. Foster, your are the president of an organization in Pittsburgh known as the Bring Home the Soldier Dead League, are you not?

Mr. FOSTER. Yes, sir.

The CHAIRMAN. When was that organization formed?

Mr. FOSTER. Some months ago, after a meeting with the Secretary of War, at which I received no satisfaction. Having met a number of parents whose sons were buried in France, and reading in the Pittsburgh and other local papers appeals from mothers especially wanting the soldier dead brought home, and realizing that there was a three-year limit put on the matter, as I understood the proclamation of the French President, I conceived the idea of getting together and having a meeting of the parents in the Pittsburgh (Pa.) district. I was able to do so by securing the use of the largest court room in the courthouse, and the press carried particular notices of the meeting. As a result of that, possibly 400 mothers and fathers attended that meeting. That was the beginning of the Bring Home the Soldier Dead League. From that time on, it has been sending propaganda throughout the country, wherever we could, but not in order to work up the sentiment, because the sentiment is already there, but in order to have the War Department realize that the parents, although there are only 50,000 or 75,000 of them, ought to be considered as much as though they numbered 700,000. As Mr. Duff said, this sentiment is growing all over the country.

The CHAIRMAN. How many people attended your last meeting in Pittsburgh?

Mr. FOSTER. I should say between five and six hundred.

The CHAIRMAN. At that meeting a committee was appointed to appear before this committee?

Mr. FOSTER. Yes, sir.

The CHAIRMAN. And you are the chairman of that committee?

Mr. FOSTER. Yes, sir.

The CHAIRMAN. And your associates on the committee are here with you?

Mr. FOSTER. Yes, sir; mothers, fathers, and widows of American soldiers who died in France.

The CHAIRMAN. Then you do not represent yourself individually, but, rather, you represent this organization known as the Bring Home the Soldier Dead League?

Mr. FOSTER. Yes, sir.

The CHAIRMAN. You may proceed with your statement.

Mr. FOSTER. We have held two meetings in Pittsburgh, and, as stated by Chairman Porter, we come to-day representing this organization, the Bring Home the Soldier Dead League. We feel that the matter has been very thoroughly covered by Gov. Montague, Col. Anderson, and Dr. Duff, and that we can not add very much to the discussion, except to say this, that we believe that the time to act is now. We do not believe that the attitude of France in demanding that a three-year period should elapse before this work shall be done should be considered at all by the American Government. These boys were taken across there when the war was at its height. We could not get them across too fast, and they went at the rate of 500,000 per month. Now, when the danger is over and the war is past, they want to hold our dead in France. We can not understand any other motive for it except that it is simply a matter of commercializing the graves of the American soldiers lying in France. As for the economic and sanitary reasons advanced, they should not have any weight whatever, because Secretary Baker himself told me that there were no sanitary reasons to prevent it now or any more than there would be three years from now. That is not the question at all. The economic situation is not such as to prevent action. The United States Government at the present time has men in France, railroads in France, and the necessary transportation at its disposal so that the work could be done very soon and could be done very quickly.

Mr. HOUGHTON. Why do you say that the American Government ought not to pay any attention to the wishes or desires of the French Government? I wish you would clear that up.

Mr. FOSTER. Because I think that the American people want the bodies of their soldier dead.

Mr. HOUGHTON. Of course I understand that; but, suppose it was true that France did object, would you have this country insist to the extent of going to war with her?

Mr. FOSTER. I do not think it would be necessary.

Mr. HOUGHTON. What I am trying to get you to say, and I think you meant to say it, but not in the blunt form in which you put it, is that this Government should do whatever it can to break down that objection.

Mr. FOSTER. Yes, sir.

Mr. HOUGHTON. It is too easy to say the other thing and give the wrong impression.

Mr. FOSTER. I think the French Government should be advised through proper channels that the mothers and fathers or next of kin of the boys who are dead in France will not submit to waiting any unnecessary period of time. Prompt action should be insisted upon, I think the whole matter can be summed up in a few words: So far as the French attitude is concerned, it is a desire to commercialize the graves of the American soldier dead. I can not see any other reason. I understand that they are building a large hotel near the Romagne Cemetery to accommodate American tourists who will be going over. They will not be the mothers, fathers, and widows of the soldiers buried there, but they will be tourists, sightseers, souvenir hunters, etc.

I have prepared a statement, which I do not care to read, but I would like to have inserted in the record. The matter has been so well stated, that it is unnecessary for me to say more. We want the Government to act now, without any further delay, and it seems to me unnecessary to wait a year or two. Many of the mothers and fathers will be dead by that time. I would like to submit this statement for the record.

(The statement referred to is as follows:)

Seventy-seven thousand American soldiers are buried in France, sacrifices to the greed of an autocratic monarch. Those heroes are our sons. Their lives went out that America might welcome home again the 2,000,000 other brave boys who came back from the inferno of the World War. We who mourn our dead can not but be thankful that a gracious Providence did not afflict 700,000 parents in place of the 70,000 or more of us who are now bowed in grief and hope. Grief for our dead, hope for your support.

It is not to the credit of America that a necessity arose for such an organization as the "Bring home the soldier-dead league," which is here represented before your honorable committee by the mothers and fathers of but a few of the hallowed and heroic dead. We are the spokesmen of a thousand parents and many other near kin who gathered at meetings in Pittsburgh recently and who realized the sinister motives which actuated France in proclaiming that our sons should remain entombed in that foreign land for at least three years. It was decided to organize a nation-wide movement to bring home the soldier dead without further delay. This is our determination, to which we have pledged our lives, our means, and our sacred honor. We look to this honorable committee to represent us in the Congress and before the administration, so that our petitions shall have its immediate sanction, that our sons' war-tired bodies may soon rest in the sacred grounds of our American cemeteries, that every parent may pay tributes of love and honor to their dust.

We were loath to believe that those in authority had any other purpose than to begin, long before now, the return of our dead to the home land; we questioned the delay, but waited. Then persons in authority began a propaganda that our dead remain in France as a shrine—a bond of friendship between America and that nation. Inspired, no doubt, by this sinister plea put out by those whose sons were returned home and who do not want to understand the depths of sorrow in our lives and hearts, the French Government by proclamation decreed that the bodies of our American soldiers would be held on foreign soil for at least three years for economic and sanitary reasons. These are not reasons, only excuses; even the strongest un-American advocates must admit their fallacy; neither will bear investigation nor support. The American press and tens of thousands of parents, wives, and near kin of the dead have expressed the real reason—commercializing the soldier dead by the French nation. This being the motive, we do now and will continue to protest until our sons have an American tomb in America for every American hero who died on foreign soil.

It has been repeatedly stated that France has over 4,000,000 dead buried in her soil, and that the removal of this immense number would stress the morale of her people to the breaking point! How about the stress of the mother-heart of America? Shall not our Nation regard the mothers who went into the jaws of death in giving birth to those sons whose sacrifice saved France and the world? But a few days ago I stood beside the casket of a mother whose son helped stem the tide of advance of the Hun horde at Belleau Wood; she patiently waited the solace of kneeling at the tomb of her son here in his native land; she had met with our league and was filled with the hope of soon having her boy. The months of waiting and uncertainty—the apparent ingratitude of her country proved too much—her physical heart lost hope with her spiritual heart. Our prayer is that she is now with her boy in that home of the soul. Alas, many other mothers are doomed to a like fate.

Over 4,000,000 dead in France! Yes; but more than 2,000,000 are French soldiers who rest in their homeland; 600,000 are British soldiers; and Britain's war policy always has been to leave her dead heroes sleep where they fall. China will insist, as is her custom, that every one of her dead is returned to his native land. Of our 77,000 dead, less than 18,000 have been destined by their next of kin to remain in France. What about the 59,000 others whose relatives have notified the War Department that they shall rest in America throughout the ages, to be shrines for unborn generations?

> It shall not be! We will not leave
> Our boys 'neath foreign sun!
> Until we bring their bodies back,
> Our best work is not done.

Mothers, demand your dead. Shall we
    Take back our word, our Nation's bond
That every one should rest
    With their loved ones in their own land?
This question is the test.
    Shall we keep faith with those who lie
A prey to tourists' crafts—
    Who search the tombs for souvenirs,
Take marks for autographs?

And when our humblest hero lies
    'Neath our own skies so blue,
The nations will respect us more
    Than to them we were true.
'Tis no question for debate—
    France shall not say us nay;
We'll bring all back, wrapped in the flag,
    Ere next Memorial Day.
We'll greet their bodies through our tears;
    Some eyes may see, perchance,
Their spirits smiling near us then,
    Our boys who died in France.

                                                DUDLEY DORN.

America, through her Government, promised every soldier who enrolled under the Stars and Stripes that in case he was called upon to make the supreme sacrifice, his body would be returned to his loved ones; this thought must have cheered our boys mightily and spurred them on to victory in many a hard-fought battle. We know the thought comforted our anxious hearts here at home. America gave that pledge unsolicited. Will America now break faith with her dead and with us? Is the three-year limit but a subterfuge that by the lapse of time we parents will have become reconciled? Did our Government tell us that after that time had passed, our dead would be brought home? No; it said this would be done at the close of the war; that time is now.

Will the millions of francs, in anticipation, poured into the coffers of the French by American tourists blind the vision of her Government or her ears to the American mother's sobs for her boy who will not return to her encircling arms and broken heart? When hard pressed by the enemy, America answered her appeals until more than 2,000,000 of our soldiers were on her battle lines; when the foe had been conquered, she urged that the Americans be sent home quickly—they were but consumers then. Those who remained as sacrifices must not be an asset to replenish an impoverished nation. Bring home the soldier dead.

I want to read into the records of your honorable committee an article printed in the Soldiers, Sailors, and Marines' Weekly News of October 18, also an editorial from the Pittsburgh Chronicle Telegraph of November 6 entitled "Commercializing our dead," and one from the Pittsburgh Dispatch of the 11th instant on "Soldiers' graves neglected," if agreeable to you gentlemen, also copies of correspondence had with the honorable Secretary of War, Mr. Baker.

Our plea is before you and we submit our just claims for your consideration and action; we would not have the mothers of your boys experience the sleepless and agonizing nights and desolate days of those grief-stricken mothers here represented; no further delay should be permitted in the return of our dead. We are confident that neither the subterfuges of France nor the unnatural attitude of Gen. Pershing, nor the machinations of governmental red tape, commonly called diplomacy, should prevail against the tear-stained, saddened eyes, upraised and wet, the lips too still for prayer, the mute despair of thousands upon thousands of mothers throughout the land.

The body of the criminal whose life is claimed by the State is returned to his family. How much more so ought that of the hero be quickly given back to his own? Is that telegram which gave us the sad news of our son's sacrifice, but which cheered us by also telling us that his body would be returned at the end of the war, to be a mere "scrap of paper," to be bandied about like Germany's treaty with Belgium? God forbid that America should procrastinate or hesitate in her duty while the mother heart is breaking!

In closing, and with no discourtesy to your honorable committee, we are impelled to ask that our demands are assured your immediate attention and support in that you will by resolution to Congress urge and insist upon the necessary representations to the French nation that we American parents will not countenance further delay in the return of our soldier dead to the homeland. By resolution, our league set the beginning of this duty not later than February 1, 1920. Every war-scarred body should be in America before next Memorial Day, so that the golden stars on our service flags may shine brighter for the knowledge that our boys are then home again.

We very respectfully submit that your recommendations are for a wholly or at least in part, civil commission to have in charge the return of our dead; the attitude of the honorable Secretary of War and of the head of the Army precludes their sincerity in securing the desire of this Nation-wide movement to bring home the soldier dead.

In the name of this delegation, officially representing western Pennsylvania and its contiguous territory, and in the name of the league of over 1,000 parents, I heartily thank your honorable committee for this hearing, and to say that any of us will be at your service in furthering our purpose.

---

227 Sixth Avenue,
McKeesport, Pa., October 6, 1919.

Dear Mr. Secretary: Please recall the interview which you had with Mrs. Foster and myself in your office on August 28, with reference to our request for authority to secure our only son's remains now buried in France; also your request that I write you about this time regarding the matter.

As you have doubtless conferred with Gen. Pershing since his reaching Washington on the subject of the return of the bodies of American soldiers now resting in France, I am writing you; this is in accord with the result of our interview.

My son, Corp. David Burton Foster, Forty-third Company, Fifth Regiment Marines, was instantly killed in action June 12, 1918, at Belleau Wood; his third burial, on June 4 last, was in the new cemetery near the town of Belleau—a picture of his grave is numbered nine in that location, as I learn from a friend at Lucy-le-Bocage.

Our request, as you may recall, is that we be permitted to go across secure our son's remains and bring them home; every cent of expense for all purposes to be borne by myself. We merely ask your written authority which will permit us to secure our son's body. I have every arrangement, as far as humanly possible, completed.

Now, Mr. Secretary, I am very familiar with practically every news item given through the press bearing on the return of our dead; the French Government's attitude, Gen. Pershing's views, etc. The latest under date line of October 4, quoting you as having "issued instructions for the Purchase, Storage and Traffic Division of the General Staff to take charge of the matter and hasten it as much as possible," in so far as those bodies interred in other countries than France are affected.

The Huns are unrepentant and are not cured of their military mania; they will again tttempt to impose their will by force across the lands now hallowed by the bodies of our sons; the thousands gathered to the north of Belleau Wood and at other cemeteries in France will, if left there by us parents and loving ones, be trampled under foot by those hordes from Germany.

I need not repeat your promises to the American people; France must not be permitted to make a show-place of what is sacred to us parents and other near kindred; to-day, even, the news items call attention to the disgraceful mania of souvenir hunters desecrating graves for trinkets; tourist concerns are advertising jaunts to places hallowed to bereaved folk such as we. This must not be; it shall not be.

I am most desirous to secure my son's body decently and with all the honor due his sacrifice; I yield the same for every other soldier's sacrifice, and would gladly help bear the burden of others, were that possible. I want your authority to go get it; I do not recognize France's position as just to the

Americans who laid down their lives on her soil, nor to America now that her immediate danger is past. I do not recognize Gen. Pershing's attitude (if he is correctly quoted) favoring the bodies remaining on French soil—or any other soil than American in the whole wide world. None of it is good enough for the least who laid down his life on any foreign ground.

Mr. Secretary, I hope to receive a favorable reply. I will secure my son's body by your authority, I trust; with no expense or effort from my own nor the French Government—merely your written direction to the proper American service in France. But, sir, without any discourtesy to you, whom I hold in high regard as a patriot and as an official, I propose to go across and get that which is most dear to Mrs. Foster, myself, and our daughters. And I believe I voice the great mass of kindred now mourning their boys who can not come back.

I do not apologize for the length of my letter—I have tried to condense my plea and argument, but I want to thank you for the very courteous interview we had in August. I sincerely hope to receive favorable attention from you, but my duty to my son must not be determined by my regard for the French restrictions nor for Gen. Pershing's recommendation. An American tomb in America for every American soldier, sailor, and marine is not demanding too much, but there shall at least be one marine brought back by his dad, and that is Burt Foster.

Thanking you again for the very pleasant interview we had, I remain,

Very sincerely, yours,

J. D. FOSTER.

The honorable the SECRETARY OF WAR,
Washington, D. C.

WAR DEPARTMENT,
Washington, October 9, 1919.

DEAR MR. FOSTER: Your letter of October 6 comes to my attention this morning. I need not tell you that I appreciate the feeling you have concerning the body of your son. Were a son of mine over there, I believe I should feel as did Col. Roosevelt and many other parents from whom word is coming to us—that the remains of their loved ones should lie beneath the fields where they fought and along the frontiers they held. But of course, I would have no right or desire to urge upon you in a matter of this sort, any conclusions other than the one which Mrs. Foster and you have reached.

For the present, however, there is no way of bringing back to America the bodies of our boys who lie in France. I indicated to you when we discussed the matter, the feeling of understanding and of certain sympathy I have for the attitude which the French Government feels compelled to take. With the dead of many nations lying beneath her soil and with five years of terrible strain fresh in the memory of her people, the Government of France fears that the procession of hundreds of thousands of bodies through the country, disinterred and en route overseas, would stress to the breaking point the morale of that nation, which has been so sorely tried since 1914. There is an additional question of the peril of an epidemic because of the sanitary difficulties involved in a task of this size and character, but I am confident that this latter objection could be surmounted, as eventually it must be.

The State Department, as you know, has made vigorous protest against the proposal for a three-year period before the disinterment and return of bodies from France might be permitted. When an agreement is reached with the French Government, the War Department will not fail to respect the wishes of those parents who wish their boys brought back, and in the meantime I am requesting the commanding general of troops in France to see that the importance of the work it is performing is impressed upon the Graves Registration Service, so that the centralized cemeteries of our dead may be fitting places for the boys who are there.

Cordially, yours,

NEWTON D. BAKER,
Secretary of War.

Mr. J. D. FOSTER,
227 Sixth Avenue, McKeesport, Pa.

STATEMENT OF MRS. GEORGE L. WALTERS, JR., PITTSBURGH, PA.

The CHAIRMAN. Mrs. Walters, you are the widow of George L. Walters, jr.?

Mrs. WALTERS. Yes, sir. I would like to speak in behalf of a very small class of women, or a very small class of people, namely, the widows and orphans of soldiers. They really represent a very illustrious type of men. The young wives and babies were probably the keenest sufferers of them all, and it is not right that the woman who paid so dearly for peace should be deprived of the opportunity to care for her husband's grave. I would like to make an appeal for that class.

The CHAIRMAN. When were you married?

Mrs. WALTERS. I was married two years before the war.

The CHAIRMAN. Your husband was a lawyer, was he not?

Mrs. WALTERS. Yes, sir; he was a lawyer, and he volunteered right at the beginning and went in as an infantry officer.

The CHAIRMAN. He went into one of the training camps, did he not?

Mrs. WALTERS. Yes, sir; into an officers' reserve training camp.

The CHAIRMAN. What was his rank?

Mrs. WALTERS. A lieutenant of infantry.

The CHAIRMAN. Of what regiment?

Mrs. WALTERS. The Thirty-fourth United States Infantry, Second Division.

Mr. DICKINSON. Did your husband ever express to you any wish or sentiment regarding the return of his body here in the event of his death in the service?

Mrs. WALTERS. My husband never assumed at all that he would not come back. He never admitted that there was any possibility of his not coming back. But I think I can answer for the young husband who went away and for the young wife. We should not be required to give our all, and I think it is only fair that we should not be made to wait. I do not see why we should be made to wait for our funerals to meet the convenience of France, because I feel keenly, just as the rest of the relatives do, that we are being deeply imposed upon by France. I really feel that we can demand that the duty of this country to us takes precedence over any consideration for France.

STATEMENT OF MR. G. A. BROOKMAN, SCOTTDALE, PA.

The CHAIRMAN. Mr. Brookman, state your occupation.

Mr. BROOKMAN. Mr. Chairman, I am not doing anything at present. I was on the police force of Scottdale. I am not going to have very much to say, any more than that I would like for you to read the letter I sent you this week. That will be all I will ask you to do.

The CHAIRMAN. All right. We will put the letter in the record.

Mr. BROOKMAN. Thank you.

SCOTTDALE, PA., *November 10, 1919.*

To the honorable Congressmen:

During our last conflict in the European war there was a call for our loved ones to go to the front in behalf of our country, and, of course, they went forward to protect our mothers and sisters from the hands of Germany's power, and sorry to say that some of them had to die an honorable death on the battle field, and their remains now lie somewhere in France. No doubt they are laid away just as good as they would be any other place, but at the same time it don't give the satisfaction to the dear ones at home that it would if they had them on their own burial lot so the relatives and friends at home could go to the grave and see it and keep it up.

Now, I would like very much to see if something can not be done to hurry back the remains. When we received the confirmation of the telegram and letters at different times from the Government we were told that they would return to us, that we could lay them away in their own towns, and at the same time we were led to believe that while the war was on that it was impossible to move them, but just as soon as the war was over that steps would be taken to bring them back—but to-day we are no wiser than we were a year ago, so we would like to see some action taken in regards to this. Our sons were good enough for Uncle Sam to take over there in the time of need, and we think we ought to have some consideration shown us in the time of sorrow.

I might go as far as to say that if the Government is not in position to handle the removal of the bodies at the present time, would it be out of place and asking too much if they would allow us to send a party with our own undertaker to bring back the remains of our loved ones who have done all they could for God and his country in time of need. I remain,

Yours, very truly,

J. A. BROOKMAN.

Mrs. H. F. Richards, of Wilkinsburg, Pa., is here. Would you like to be heard, Mrs. Richards?

Mrs. RICHARDS. I will only take a couple of minutes of your time.

STATEMENT OF MRS. H. F. RICHARDS, OF WILKINSBURG, PA.

Mrs. RICHARDS. Chairman Porter, gentlemen, and Representatives of Foreign Affairs, we have left our homes to come here before this committee with a plea that the bodies of our soldier boys be removed from France as quickly as possible and brought back to our own United States of America for Christian burial. We love our country. We bow with reverence to our own Stars and Stripes of Old Glory. Our boys fought under the flag and died that it still might float over all of the Union.

They did their bit and did it well. History has recorded their names on its martyr roll. Will our own United States of America lower her standard? I do not believe it. She will ring true. She will bring our boys back. And, gentlemen, you, as our Representatives, we plead with you as only mothers and wives can do; hasten the work; commence at once; every mother who has lost a son in this broad land of ours is back of you with her prayers. Let the bodies all be brought home at one time, with the caskets on board a dozen or more transports, if necessary.

Let the precious freight composed of our dear boys be escorted across the Atlantic Ocean by every available fighting ship in the American Navy, including the destroyers. Let an invitation be extended to the English, French, and Italians to send naval vessels to join the escorting column. Let the funeral trip to America be made by the greatest armada that ever sailed the seas. Do this, gentlemen, to impress upon the world that America has not forsaken her heroic dead, because of a nation that our noble boys gave their lives for, in the victorious campaign that drove out the German invader. If you do this. it will be recorded in the history of our country as the greatest, biggest, grandest feat in its national history. Do you catch the vision? Do you realize what it all would mean? And best of all, it would be the keeping of the faith with our boys now sleeping on foreign soil.

We, as members of this committee, will face the executive and administrative branches of the Government with the same determination that our boys faced the bullets and disease overseas.

Our cause is right and just and God is on His throne, and we will win.

The promise we made our boys He will help us to keep.

I want to say just here that a year ago to-day our only boy lay dying in France. You gentlemen, as men and fathers, all know what that means, and I want to say that I do appreciate the courtesy of Mr. Porter and this committee in extending this invitation to us to let us come and put this matter before you.

I thank you all.

The CHAIRMAN. Gentlemen, Col. Pierce is here, but it is now 12 o'clock, and I assume that most of you desire to go down to the House. I am rather anxious to have placed in the record what England is doing on this question and what France is doing. Col. Pierce says that he can put in writing just as easily as he could tell it orally.

Mr. DICKINSON. Can you not just make a brief statement, Colonel?

Col. PIERCE. I can state it in a few sentences.

The CHAIRMAN. Then we will hear you now.

Col. PIERCE. The British Government some time ago, a year and a half ago, created what they call the Imperial War Graves Commission, which has the Prince of Wales as the honorary president and Gen. Weir, the director general of the British Graves Registration Service, as practically the working member, because his service has all the records and the cemeteries under their control. A third member is Mr. Rudyard Kipling, and the rest of the membership comprises some of the most eminent citizens of the Empire. That is the working body which practically decides all questions, and while England is not expecting to return her dead to their homes at all—it has always been the British policy that they shall lie where they fell—yet at the same time there is a vast work to be done all over Europe and part of Asia in reference to establishing or perfecting their cemeteries. They are planning to do a great work, and their campaign involves a period of some six years.

You asked also about France. France, likewise, has a commission which is headed by Gen. Castelnau, the third ranking general of the French Republic, coming next after Marshal Petain, and he is the head of what they call the French National Commission on Military Sepulchers. I have the honor, by the way, to be one of the American members of that commission for consultation in connection with such features as pertain to the French mortuary work and our own work in common. Many times we encounter the bodies or the graves of French dead, and sometimes they encounter the bodies or graves of American dead, and we have an interchange of information and an exchange of services, and we are all working together; in fact, all the armies of the Allies have been working together to produce the best possible results in the care of the dead, because the dead of all the Allies are our dead, as the fight was ours, and the ideals were ours, and the resulting civilization is our common possession.

Mr. BROWNE. I would like to ask Col. Pierce one question. Colonel, could that work be begun right at the present time, safely and properly, so far as sanitary conditions are concerned.

Col. PIERCE. I think so. I do not think that the American people or the American surgeons have at any time given a very great deal of consideration to the sanitary argument. I think they have all felt that the precautions we were able to take would prevent any bad results.

Mr. BROWNE. Another question: Do you think we could remove all of our dead from France in a year's time if we went at it the way we ought to?

Col. PIERCE. I presume, sir, that would be a difficult question for any man to answer positively, but a year, in my judgment, would be rather a small period of time to set. There are many things to be considered, for instance, our ability to get the caskets we should need. This is just a practical difficulty, but just now we are providing between 4,500 and 5,000 in order to carry out the project which I outlined to the committee once before, the removal of our dead from all countries except France, and we shall not be able to secure that small number of caskets within three months.

Now, that is less than 5,000 as against 75,000. The matter of procurement will cut some figure, the matter of transportation may cut some figure, the matter of training personnel may cut some figure. I have a good many of my men who were with us in Europe now lined up and waiting for appointment to go back there for the portion of the project that has already been placed in our hands. If we can get a sufficient number of those men who are acquainted with the conditions on these foreign fields as well as technically proficient, like embalmers, undertakers, and others, there is no telling what we might accomplish. I think it would be our object to work with the utmost speed consistent with safety, but, first of all, I think that all the relatives of the dead ought to be urged not to allow the consideration of speed to operate as against the condition of safety. We want, when we come to you to say, "This is the body of your boy." We stand back of the name marked on the casket that we bring to you. We expect, in many cases, you are going to open those caskets, or you are going to have somebody do it—pray God, you may not do it yourselves, but when you do, we want to present to you only that which will be corroborative of what we say ourselves, and we must not be pressed to the point of speeding up so that we are going to sacrifice safety and have a little shifting of our eyes when you look at us. We want to look you squarely in the eye and we want you to believe our word and we want to be able to prove up on it after we have made our statements.

The CHAIRMAN. Are there any further questions?

Mrs. WALTERS. Mr. Porter, is it possible to have an expression of opinion as to whether it will be possible for people to do this privately, for instance, for an individual to send a man over to bring back their soldier dead?

The CHAIRMAN. I think that is a matter for later consideration. It is possible we can arrange with the War Department to have some representative present——

Col. PIERCE (interposing). There again, Mr. Chairman, it is a question largely of personnel, because you would not want your Government to give consent to have just anybody go to a cemetery and open up a grave. We must have our own representative there to see that the right grave is opened and so on.

Mr. FOSTER. We would not want to submit that at all.

Col. PIERCE. No.

The CHAIRMAN. I think that is a matter for consideration later.

(The committee thereupon adjourned.)

X

Printed by Libri Plureos GmbH in Hamburg, Germany